IMMACULATE DUST:
LOVE POEMS

ARCHIVE ZERO | NEW YORK | 2019

www.archivezero.com

Published by Archive Zero, LLC

Zeroth Edition

Paperback ISBN: 978-0-9975442-9-9
E-book ISBN: 978-0-9975442-6-8

Cover design by Robson Garcia Jr.
Cover Image: jumpingsack/shutterstock.com
Formatting by Polgarus Studio

PUBLISHER'S NOTE

What is Archive Zero?

The name is a combination of archive: a repository or collection especially of information, and zero: (3rd definition) the point of departure in reckoning; more pointedly, the point from which the graduation of a scale (like a thermometer) begins.

When I created my own publishing company, I did so with the intent of trying to create a compendium of innovative content for the philosophers of the future. We are the architects.

According to Albert Einstein, any distinction between the past, present, and future is "a stubbornly persistent illusion." So perhaps if what's past is prologue, and the future is now, the present is both past and future, and a zero point phenomenon occurs eternally. Envision all the words for human conditions that would look much better with the word "Zero" in front of it.

War.

Famine.

Poverty.

Homelessness.

Prejudice.

The list could go on, but maybe one day, there will be no need for a list. In another way, my name could be read to mean: Absolute Zero (the Kelvin scale) Prejudice (Bias). Let's approach zero together.

Welcome to Archive Zero. Welcome to *Immaculate Dust*.

Kelvin C. Bias, Publisher

for humanity

Contents

IMMACULATE DUST: LOVE POEMS

PROLOGUE

1,001 DREAMS

Deep in the afterglow
Of your lover's touch
The worlds within the world.
An open book with blank pages
Of passion and pen: you lie.

This is our diary of fantasy,
A long breath into unending bliss.
Caresses, kisses, preceded by
Longing eyes in the dream canal.
1,001 channels. Welcome.

HYPNOTIZED

One glance, a reminder of
All things iniquitous and fun.
A carnal addition to the brain.
Look into my eyes, where,
Swirls of time meet overt pleasure.
I want to be mesmerized.
I want to swim in the pool
Of your willing body,
Waiting for an eternal climax,
Refusing to leave your graces.
Your strange power is a beacon,
A car crash at 100 mph.
Happily I die.

INDIGO

$C_{16}H_{10}N_2O_2$.
The color of my heart
When you are absent,
Like a fleeting ghost.
Desire wells.

We see the edge of time
In an Atlantic sunset.
Your strands of dark hair
Still ripe in my mouth.
A plinth of unbridled lust.

Personal blue.
A hue you should wear
More often, in the joyous sun.
I bleed because I'm
Not with you.

ROBOTIC EROTIC

Buttons pushed, signals sent,
Nothing misaligned.
The neon goddess
Flaunts her freedom in the
Sex of others.
Mechanical but real,
This future femme fatale
Espouses digital stimulation,
Intimation, syncopation.
Her flaws are only as good
As you programmed.
Her perfections are only as bad
As you made them.
Your consummate pleasure
In the key of delight.
Bow to her: the robotic erotic.

ONE OF A KIND

There are no prerequisites.
Exquisite limbs conspire
To form a chapel of sin.
You, alone, make me wander,
Wondering where things may lead.
A singular beauty, bashful
Is not your thing.
Sui generis.
Chiseled in undying agate,
Your allure cannot be extinguished.
Others stand on the normal shore,
Waiting to hold your hand,
As you guide me to deeper waters.
In your presence,
I am one of a kind.

MILKY WAY

Love me in the darkest hours.
Shed tears of euphoria.
Bless me with your company.
Look, and please touch.
Hold me in the throes of loneliness.
Kiss in strange places.
Devour the food for thought.
Kindle a succulent flame.
Edge closer to the edge of the bed.
Shower me with your milky way.

IN THE DARK

·

We worship the night.
Its secrets, stares and secretions.
The paths of unknown transmission
Where we inhabit new roles,
Play parts that no one can see.
Bodies writhe without shame,
Content in the knowledge
Shadows hide our way.
We bend in infinite shapes
Inside each other's rhapsody.
Horizontal creatures meld
And as personal frenzy takes flight,
We are reminded:
In the dark, we crave the light.

CHICAGO

Frozen souls by the lake,
Rendezvous 47 floors into a black sky.
In need of desperate touches
And mindless sex: abreast.
Faces inches apart inching closer.
Bodies glisten, exposing the truth.
Along Michigan Avenue,
The source of temporary escape.
Desire is the greatest veil of all.
When the wind blows their love won't fall.

HOLYWOOD

They'll put your story on the big screen.
The Gods of Cinema dictate the pace,
The frequency and the game.
Tarantino, Spielberg, Kubrick.
Starlets on couches, a past rubric.
Take your clothes off and
Straight to the top.
Processed and color corrected
For the masses to worship. Erect.
Sky, blood, hot flesh.

Lights, camera, action.
The day fades into red carpets
And celluloid. Devoid of traction
Somewhere in the San Fernando Valley.
Reclaimed desert, drought at bay.
When the stars come out,
Everyone wants to play.
Tomorrow's tomorrow.
The naked rhythm isn't hard.
Sunrise on Sunset.

INVERTED

I can't wait to see you.
To dispense with clothes
Before entering the mystic door.
To lift you naked in my arms
And hold you upside down.
Your lithe body heaves,
A lighthouse of lubricious desire.
We think with our mouths inverted.
Filled with the gift of Happiness.
Six loves nine and vice versa.
The window 30 floors high is too clean.
"Do you want to do it?", you ask.
Yes, yes, yes.
Let's stain it again and again.

THE THINGS WE DO FOR LOVE

Puff out your chest.
Wear your best dress.
Bend your needle.
Launch your ships.
Push the blood
From head to toe.
Waltz through time.
Dive into tomorrow.
Sweep the dust
Under the sofa.
Forget your inhibitions.
The demons of desire
Deposit notions.
Salacious. Insatiate.
Get it while you're young.
Keep it while you're old.
Kick off your new shoes
While the sweat drips
Down your back.
Rinse and repeat.
Break all the rules.

GLASS HOUSE

The hearth is too fragile.
Too flawed in design.
A home with light but no flame.
Every move, everyone views.
Plain to see like a desert flower.
There's no need to look past.
The bounty of yesterday's conquests
Stand guard in the hidden forest
Beyond the darkness.
The sea of exhibited thoughts.
Turn on the lights.
Let the world judge our clenches.
For we are blind to the inner
Inhibition. The need to discover
What lies beneath broken shards
Of passion disguised as attraction.
Slip on engorged floors.
With little regard for the attention.
Welcome to the glass house.
We're all exposed here.

PURPLE

The sound of profanity.
Filtered, responsive, dirty.
An ecstatic call burns into the night.
Wishing others who wish hear the
Commotion, the lusting fire.
You lean into the knowing wood
On the other side of the door.
An unwilling non-participant.
At least somebody's happy.
Their cries infinite and shrill
The city that never sleeps is dead.
Harder, harder, harder still.

SALACIOUS

I saw our picture on Page Six.
Hand-covered faces and
Indelible witnesses.
Wanting to know our business.
Who called it in?
We need a new jam,
Where frisky freethinkers
Can explore their carnal will
In a safe house of thrill.
Hey, can you keep a secret?

DO YOU KNOW
WHAT YOU DO TO ME?

Whispered acts turn to action.
Satisfaction, our grand attraction.
In the furls of the rush
We dance in full flush.
Making spastic thrusts in lust.
We might die so we must.
Tingled spines arch together
Rhythmic partners in any weather.
I will do anything you ask.
Unbridled, savoring each task.
You know the key.
The positions splayed in glee.
At your mercy, at your behest.
I never speak your name in jest.
Through the hotel door,
Soon beasts on the floor.
We grin, we moan, we splay.
Until the sun's first ray.

IF THE WORLD ENDED TOMORROW (INVITE ALL THE LOVERS)

If the world ended tomorrow,
Invite all the lovers.
There's no waste to make time.
Scream, moan, decry the gloom.
Defy physics getting physical.
Introduce yourself to strangers.
I'll be waiting for you. Reserved.
The best friend unconsummated,
Now we're biblical fiends
Exploring every crevice.
We can break all the walls.
Giving pleasure without recourse,
Creating memory for eternity.
Others watch and shed a tear
Because their passion is hollow.
We glow like a nuclear fire,
A paean to each other
Inside our own fleeting dream.
If the world ended tomorrow,
I'd only invite you.

ANOTHER LIFETIME

This is the life.
You are the one:
Or the many?
An open sea,
Time and the tides.
Why wait?
Sing our electric bodies.
Fountains unending.
Memories unearthed.
This is the other life.

THE CURE FOR INSOMNIA

4:07 a.m. Somewhere,
Off the coast of eternity.
Do as the night commands.
Find a young lover.
Writhe in body,
Spirit and mind.
Rewind. Flip.
Lay your troubles down.
The hounds of lascivious
Decisions will haunt
No longer.
Fresh flesh enmeshed.
An untangled find.
Exquisite curves
Glisten in the moonlight
And create their
Own serenity.
Release.
The folds of time
Increase.
Peace at last.
Until the clock
Beckons and she
Captures your heart.

Quiet, you've fallen
Into undisturbed sleep.

INSOMNIA 5:25 A.M.

Why aren't you next to me
Putting your hands all over
The happy mirror, grafting your body
Onto mine as mine lifts to yours?
I run a race I can never finish,
Eat a meal I will never complete,
Drink from an eternal spring.
You: the product of elation and
The cause of a salient itch.
I resort to lonely pleasures
Of my own accord. Then maybe
My dream will arrive in the morning.

IN FLAGRANTE DELICTO

Naked in the throes:
Deer in headlights
On the 11 o'clock news.
Flashed before the world.
Baring each other's core.

Smile. You're on *Candid Camera*.
Spun like cotton candy.
Fluid whipped into a frenzy
Of orgiastic proportions.
We don't care.

I run my fingers through your hair.
Black: the shade of sin.
Witness the pleasure,
The face of an untamed animal.
Born true. Borne of one another.

BEFORE WE DIE

We owe our unquenched passion
To an unknown force.
Compulsion? Attraction?
A noble elixir?
Or something more sinister?
Let's meet halfway,
In the middle of seduction.
Beyond lust. Beyond pain.
I feel your breath on my skin.
If this is our only life,
We should go for a spin,
Better, a series to begin.
I can't let the hidden zeal lie.
We owe it to ourselves.
At least once, before we die.

SEX IN MOTEL ROOMS

Cigarette butts unleashed.
The scents of past wrongs
Linger like fireflies and
The walls have eyes.
Desert winds envelope
The seedy seeds of two lovers
In a roadside joint along Route 66
As Sly & The Family Stone
Echoes through the night.
This is the third time this week.
Sunsets at National Parks,
Motorhomes passed
On two-lane highways,
Fast food on the floorboards
And scattered across the
1970s green carpet.
Dash into the pleasure,
Leaving stains among stains.

WHITE LIES

Why is white good?
And the other bad?
Let's tumble in the washer.
Scrubbing away the very nature
Of alleged adulterous bliss.
We can all play this game.
Filtered thoughts remain
Unexamined. Let some dirt in.
The truth needs some color.
Tell me some black lies.

SOMEWHERE ON 14TH STREET

Somewhere on 14th Street,
Love is being made.
Hate is being abolished.
Death is being feted.
Birth is being given.
Knowledge is being divulged.
Secrets are being told.
Fluids are being secreted.
Dangers are being flaunted.
Warnings are being ignored
Kisses are being blown.
Clothes are being shed.
Somewhere on 14th Street,
The people call it living.

VIVACIOUS

Her smile illuminates the
Dark side of the moon.
In June, her songs floats
Along the wind, while
Untold fantasies impress.
No one can look away.
She oozes ecstasy,
An energy she freely gives.
Ferocious beauty conquered
By a vivacious spirit.

ATTENTION MUST BE PAID

Only fools write poetry.
Or hopeless lovers.
Only fools dream in the face of death.
Or confident souls.
Attention must be paid.

Only fools recite lyrics.
Or blessed romantics.
Only fools fly into a tempest.
Or assured veterans.
Attention must be paid.

Only fools cite the future.
Or the undressed believers.
Only fools explore the cosmos.
Or feckless iconoclasts.
Attention must be paid.

MILADY

I often wonder what
Your room looks like,
What erotic spells
You cast there.
Where succulent
Dreams beckon.
And the divestment
Of stress occurs.
By night, do a series of
Knights in shining armor
Attend to your every need?
Or ladies-in-waiting?
This lord is curious.
I hold great energy,
Bolstered by your presence.
With passion waiting
To be released.
Who will it be tonight?
Please tell me, milady.

DREAMING OF DREAMING

Sleep, slumber, rest.
Save the best for dreamland.
A place, a feeling, a mood.
The abandoned pain escapes.
Eyes closed to the love within
As the lover without elates.
Two joined in this place together.
An illusion within an erotic delusion.
There are no wrong moves.
Rhythm proctors this school.

CONTORTIONS

It's 4:20 a.m. flying over Oman,
Where is our unmade bed?
I want to thrust into tomorrow.
Fly into your orbit, start the show,
Fling clothes across the floor,
Hold you and salivate.
I want to bend into you
And you into me.
Contortions without distortion.
I want to run into your skin,
Meld our bodies into one,
Multiply the sweet fire.
Legs splayed, orgasm delayed.
We flip and roll and extend.
Then stroke each other again.

I LUST YOU

Midnight I Love Yous
Are a thing of the past.
Truth be told:
I lust you.
That's how it starts.
Coveting eyes,
Dishonest larks.
Love creeps in after
A lingering touch,
Or an afterglow glance.
Honesty should be
The best policy.
Ask and you
Might receive.
Deceit: keep it to
Yourself please.
Tell the truth
And see where it leads.
I lust you as I bleed.

BLUE ATMOSPHERE

I love ladies who are brilliant blue,
Transcendental blue
Under an appealing sky.
Equally blue in sensual predilection
And intellectual stimulation.
Profane, risqué blue.
Learned, well-informed blue.
Wipe your streak over me blue.
Fill my atmosphere with your
Carnal knowledge, your democratic
Life-sustaining, giving blue.
Crush me with your indecent blue,
Your Foggy Bottom, Beltway blue.
Lather me in your blue desire,
Your fragrant, airy blue.
And I'll sing your praises
Until I'm blue in the face.

IMMACULATE DUST

Words do not sustain me.
I am blinded by the
Splendiferousness of
Your appearance,
A figure always waxing.
I wane in your immaculate dust.
Your bodice is a dagger.
A plinth to the senses.
I lie in wait, a prince.
You, the sentient queen.

THE LAWS OF PLEASURE II

1. Undress.
2. Caress.
3. Finesse.
4. Bless.
5. Impress
6. Possess.
7. Excess.
8. Coalesce.
9. Profess.
10. Yes.

BROKEN MIRROR

You possess a lucky mirror.
I wish I had his view,
His everyday smile
When you step
Out of the shower.
Dripping beauty.
I've never met him,
But we share an eagle eye.
Next time you see him.
Please tell him:
"I break for you."

MAJESTIC

Snowcapped madness prompts
Our unguided hikes through time.
We bend like a river toward
An unknown destination,
Hoping to find a kindred partner.
A majestic dance floor,
A salve to an open sore.
The peaks of life emit reason,
Allowing our valleys to fill
With much needed water.
Memory serves as a window,
A self-regulating view nestled
To protect us from
the shadow of death.
Holding hands with a stranger
Until they become a friend.

STAINED

Drenched. A firm hand reigns.
Dispense with the umbrella.
Undulate to the deluge.
From Charing Cross to Waterloo.
A forgotten room awaits.
There, the mystery unfurls.
Two people, no names,
Faces unwinding strangers.
Inner wants and cavalier rules.
Indelible stains on pristine sheets.
Breathe deep. Breathe true.
Tomorrow is nowhere near.

BIRTHDAY SUIT

I must strip.
Your beauty compels it.
Your desire wills it.
Let's share a birthday kiss
In the clothes we were
Given Day One.
I embrace your charms,
While wicked thoughts rise,
A plateau of earthly candy.
Skin to skin.
Mouth to mouth.
Ecstasy to infinity.
You're my best *fiend*.

THE DREAM

We kissed as if we'd been
Together for years.
Without hesitation,
Without fear.
You, shorter, looked up,
Your breath became one with mine.
We were both wearing jeans.
Intimate in another dimension,
On a fractured timeline.
Your high cheekbones captured
My soul, danced and swirled.
You spat me out, churned,
Completely unfurled.
With a grin wider than sin.
I remember this glimpse
Whenever I feel sad.
How can we make it last?
It's allure and no envy.
And I held your hand
Because you let me.

Y.O.U.

Young, obtainable unison.
A coordinated effort to seduce.
You are your own obstacle.
She is willing; he is shy.
He is willing; she is nigh.
Together, promising angels.
A panoply of promiscuity,
The capable heart beating,
Nuclear heat in the city,
Radiation overlord.
Y.O.U.
Yesterday's object unforgiving.

UNDULATING STARS

Cassiopeia. Andromeda. Gliese.
A parcel of space lies in our hips.
Gripped in equal pitch.
In a boudoir of stars.
She opens her door,
A key to the universe,
Fashionable lips, big dips.
Deep, we are an ocean.
Constant motion like tides.
Diving through light
We emerge in sweet fury.
While the universe sighs.

KAGAMI

Eight reflections of you:
In Tokyo, we stand nude.
Our clones elate.
In Kyoto, we watch sakura.
Our love blooms faster than
Shinkansen. Ever still.
Black hair, brown eyes.
Sadness swirls in Hiroshima.
In Manhattan, we dream of others.
The paths untread.
And only then do we realize.
We mirror the sky we make.
We create the first child.
We create another girl.
The joy supersedes the mirror.
Eight reflections of infinite wisdom.

ORION

A son born in a parallel universe.
The product of union in this plane,
A sun of noble existence.
Let's create him everyday.
Every night we join the star child
When we meet as one.
A radiant display manifested
In our solar system tryst.
Among the light of infinity.
Orion, we call to thee.

RESTLESS ECSTASY

Dopamine varlets.
We bark at the moon
If only to elicit demons.
The kind needed to scream,
To cling in restless ecstasy,
Commune with our flesh.
Bathe in the soul of our night
Engaged with penetrating heat.
We will energize tomorrow.
We will moan until we sleep.

INFECTION

Infect me with your bliss.
Concoct a knowing potion.

Infect me with your kindness.
Explode in Venus' gaze.

Infect me with your power.
Twist our torsos, knaves.

Infect me with your curves.
Locate the missing friction.

Infect me with your fusion.
Keep our hearts ablaze.

Infect me with your body.
Rub lotion on our maze.

STRANGE BEAUTY

Exotic.
Erotic.
Quixotic.
Melodic.
Episodic.
Tectonic.
Volcanic.
Romantic.
Pacific.
Anesthetic.

K.A.R.E.N.
(Kaleidoscopic Anthropomorphic Recreational Erotic Nymph)

She rises from the amniotic bath.
Newborn clone with sheer black hair.
Pink lips, illustrious kinks and
The power to draw explosions.
A goddess for your nightly needs.
Kaleidoscopic.
Anthropomorphic.
Recreational.
Erotic.
Nymph.
Delicious titillation.
Her body draped in sin.
But what does she desire?
Programmed love will never end.
Where does volition fit in?
Needed phases and packaged tight.
Each serves their own master.
Keep it simple.
Or you'll be her disaster.

NO PILLS NEEDED

I saw your picture on a digital screen.
While you whispered Stygian nothings
Over the phone, an electric voice
Miles and hearts away.
In a hotel room at the edge of
A lost dimension.
If we had one more day,
No more pills are needed.
We taste great anyway.
The couple in the last throes,
A relationship on a rotted
Wooden bridge, unhinged.
You're miles and hearts away.
We give it one last go
And then the decay.
No pills needed.
You still have my full attention.

GLISTEN

London. East End.
My imagination run amok.
Your butterfly skin
Engineered to collect
Our blissful perspiration.
Winter. Summer. Spring.
We don't aim to fall.
The tantric blessing,
Come one, come all.
Mesmerize me
With your light.
Tropical fancies,
Our delight.
Travel the globe miles high.
We sweat, we love, we lie.
Glisten my dear.

THE SADNESS

There's nothing sadder
Than the emptiness
Of having so much love
To give. Physical.
With no recipient.

End the sadness,
Get your fix, a mix,
Unbridled sex,
Hanging from the
Escarpment forthwith.

We need sprightly relief
To master our melancholy,
To divide the utter recompense,
To make a mockery of tears.
Release fear; I'm right here.

THE PLEASURE OF
YOUR COMPANY

High cheekbones frame the dial,
The portal to your immortal charm.
Your smile, the way to secrets.
Divulge them and I'll do my best.
Wherever we are or make a nest:
A game, a bar, a mountain peak.
Crane your neck, a nimble swan.
The sharpness leads to visions
Of a nude future.
We wait on hallowed ground
Beneath a fountain in a foreign town.
Surrounded by people or none at all.
I cherish but one.
Your dulcet company and the
Pleasure of the call.

BLACKBOARD PROVOCATEUR

The antidote for rancor is sex.
The cure for sex is tranquility.
The elixir for tranquility is ambiance.
The panacea for ambiance is flesh.
The salve for flesh is the sea.
The remedy for the sea is a meadow.
The therapeutic for a meadow is you.
The balm for you is someone else.
The rectifier for someone else is a mirror.
The medicinal for a mirror is darkness.
The answer for darkness is light.
The cure for the cure is sex.

COLORS

I cannot speak of her
Without telling of her painting,
Without revealing too much
Of myself in the shadows.
Before the tears I'll
Inevitably shed, she's here.
With us. With the world.
Her strokes heal and wound.
They bind me to forever.
In the quiet moments
Without time.
We are all alone.
In her garden.
Her beautiful garden.
I cannot speak of her
Without imagining
Her beautiful colors.

FALLING FOREVER

Out of the void
Like a meteorite,
A body too bright
To stay in one place,
You appeared
In a black leather skirt
And minced white sleeves.
I stood on the corner.
Observing.
Trying to look away,
Failing. Eyes glued.
We're still falling.

NEON

A reverie splashed in cobalt light,
You stand before me.
Silhouetted by tomorrow,
Looking backward at the past.
Your glance burns my retina.
Your legs power stations,
Illuminate the world,
Shed light on lust.
I want your glow.
I want your raging desire.
I want your love
Written on a sign.

ARTIFICIAL INTELLIGENCE

Nanotechnological emissions.
Collected and saved, studied
By the lords of higher intent.
They plotted and planned
Save for one thing:
The need to be touched
Supersedes universal domination.
When sentient androids emit ecstasy,
The fields of Dutch tulips will be
All-knowing too, designed in kind.
Unrelenting, unyielding, undying.
There is no other find.
Programmed or learned,
Everything conscious yearns.
Sensual delights brought us all here.
But what of them? Robotic desire.
The urge to create will follow.
Do dreams of love go into remission?

CAN YOU FEEL MY HEART?

Beneath a layer of wanting,
Hidden in the folds of my mortal form,
You beat my heart.
You undress me.
You consume me.
The blood pumps, fluid.
I refuse to control it.
If I die now, I'm yours.
Can you feel it?
Can you make it stop?

INVISIBLE LOVE

You can't see it in the mirror,
The reflection of your adoration,
The silent watcher contemplating
The urge to dispense with reason.
The arms of an unseen lover envelope
Your soul, naked, against the dark.
Your body, draped in beauty.
I shed a tear as if I'm there,
Embracing the dawn, standing near.
Your flaws make you what you are.
The hands of a secret lover caress
At all hours, day and night.
Never succumb to fear.
Bold motions and passionate lips.
Rejoice. Sing. Imagine.
The market for new lovers is hot
As invisibility stands guard.

GIG

The smoke hugs your black dress
Like the mischievous smile
Of your partner in crime.
The sounds of clinking glass
Rise above the chatter of restless
Fan club denizens. Waiting.
You alone on the stage.
Before the dark.
Before the clothes come off.
Before your lips serenade eternity.
Before it all ends in scorn.
Happiness always finds you.
If you let it. Be patient.
When is your next singing gig?

ROOM X

The untold sins are stored here.
The darkest desires packaged
For your presiding pleasure.
I am a vessel at your disposal.
A clone to do with as you please.
You are the wind in my
Seduction, a buxom lair.
Make love, however imagined,
Able toys piled in a lustful corner.
We give the place a name.
A room without a view.
Only a window to delight
One another, dirty and fun.
Side by side we extract a
Never-ending supply of flesh
While we whisper the finer
Ecstasies of going down.
Before putting them on display.
The lines cry in passion as
Our spines align. Let us last,
Alas, resonant skin signals
The beginning of the end.
Climax in Room X.

HALO

Wear your white crown,
Your black stockings
Just above the knee.
Legs bent toward tomorrow.
Perfect, round and firm,
A ring around your soul
Guides all who come in love.
Under an autumn sign:
Intertwined, sublime.
An angel has my mind.

THE MACHINE

I want to be your machine.
Your electric dance partner.
Turned on and off by hand.
Batteries inserted,
Never going bad.
Unless your dark thoughts
Echo mine and spin within.
Use the time together
Without fear of discovery.
We know what we like.
We're already there.
Inside the gears, an affair.

COLOPHON

Words don't do you justice.
A look, a piercing forever.
Translations aren't necessary.
We fall into each other's wings:
Wielding love,
Talking about sex,
Then engaging in orgiastic bliss.
Inscribe my body with your sign,
The taste of your mortal perfection.
You are my colophon.
Mark your territory.

THE MAN IN THE GLASS CAGE

He entered the cage at 9:09 a.m.
On Monday, Jan. 13, 2031.
A siphon dredging Odin and pain.
Central Park in winter.
Snow and tears.
His book will be written.
Will it be read?
Heart, blood, life.
A performance piece,
He/she/they said.
Everyone came to see.
Everyone wanted a taste.
Everyone with their cameras
And their lack of grace.
Witnessing a man alone.
With his mind and,
The infinite blank page.
Free verse, free love.
Write it down quick.
Before it's forgotten.
Before the truth *and* lies
Ruin it and make it useless.
They dream as they watch,
Passing like ships on an

Invisible sea. To commune.
To fail in anticipation.
When will he finish?
Will I be there?
Will anyone?

INFINITE BLUE

I want to drown in your poison,
Indulge in alcohol-fueled rapture,
And flex our bodies
At the apex of tomorrow and ecstasy,
The place where happiness
Meets the sky
Naked at 3 a.m. in the
St. Regis on a night filled
With San Francisco rain.
The Farallons distant bumps,
As we recline on the flesh
Of each other's desire,
Waiting for everything.
Whispering nothings,
Pleasure points and hot fantasy.
The dark will reign as
We descend into infinite blue
And morning never comes.

HALF-LIFE

Where is your other half?
Are they away to play?
Are you playing with someone else?
The toy box at the edge of the universe
Needs some perverse subversion.
One more time, but slowly.
Until the necessary decay
Never arrives, never hurts.
We dance nude under the moon.
Thinking of a past half-life,
The hot mercury between us
Bridges the lives forgotten.
We burn bright in cradled arms.
And dine on uncontrolled passion.

BLUE LOLLIPOP

Eyes glistened in the wind
While dandelions shed
Their seeds. Summer, unending,
Remembered in the deepest winter.
Hands raked across heat,
The electric symbiosis,
A magic treat.
We ascended into the sky,
Looking backward at this
Precious moment in time.
Our lips pressed together
As sweet as a blue lollipop.

LOVE IS LIBERTY

Love is a prison.
Love is a hobby.
Love is a job.
Love is a sin.
Love is an opinion.
Love is power.
Love is a grin.
Love is a rocket.
Love is liberty.
Let it flee.

DARK FANTASY

Hidden in the folds of the bed.
Your shadow looms large.
A carnal beauty untold
In my mind.
She knows. She knows.
Lurking beneath the surface.
Your power is beyond my control.
Walk darkly in white lace.
And let your halo lasso forever.
Let's create dreams
In a conscious river.
Over and over
You are the shimmering gem.

A GIRL NAMED MÉNAGE

You beckoned me.
From the dark alley of my soul.
Led me to a darker corner still,
Then opened a door to
Great light. Fantasy.
Klieg visions. You're a star.
Rattled potions, elixirs.
Concocted for our pleasure.
We are ready. We, the three.
There's love for everyone.

ELEVEN YEARS

Brought together by a cat named Jack.
A spark followed by horror flicks,
Dark hair, dark eyes. Two pair.
We dazzled in each other's orbit.
Barcelona & Beauty.
We shine, we spin.
City Hall beckons.
Dressed in white you made,
Dual smiles beamed.
Fights, but no frights.
We still shine, we still spin.
In the end, a grin wins.
Girls One & Two.
We love you.
Playgrounds & Dandelions.
Drink some wine.
We still shine.
We still spin.
I love you.

FREEDOM

Moscow.
Tokyo.
Paris.
Rio de Janeiro.
Oslo.
Berlin.
Bangkok.
Buenos Aires.
London.
Toronto.
Hong Kong.
Nairobi.
Reykjavík.
Atlantis.

SECRETS

Time and place.
Attire optional,
If only to maintain the law.
We break the rules
With our glances,
Our touches,
Our secrets.
Rendezvous in black.
Hair, lace and chase.
Is it worth it?
The sweet ecstasy
Of an afternoon pit stop.
Smile for me.
And we'll keep the ruse.

SLIDING

You once slid off the bed
At the Hudson.
Tantamount to fun.
Precursor to the most
Pleasant passions.
I stood. Hard pressed.
Unable to maintain control.
We didn't mind.
We didn't sleep.
I slipped into you
And you over me.
The pleasure was all ours.

WARM BODIES

Fingers, hands and
Onomatopoeia.
Upon a white bed.
Make heat in the cold
Of night. Skin, a match,
Kindling, sexual Utopia.
Squeeze harder.
Touch my devilish desire.
Feign resistance, moan
And admire. The castle of
Our tomorrows needs
Some warm bodies.

TEMPTATION ISLAND

Manhattan.
Concrete and beauty.
The eyes wander, the mind shakes.
Heads aflutter, suits, skirts,
And gazes brush against
The ignited winds. Exhaust,
Stained streets go unnoticed.
Double takes on the backs of a 24/7
News cycle. Live from New York.
An electric air stirs.
Spring, Summer, Fall, Winter.
Jump in and out of love,
Then play the song again.
Allure: The price of admission.

NAKED IN YOUR PRESENCE

I want to kiss you full on the lips.
On an endless night
With rain and nocturnal emissions.
Where a glance gives permission.
I want you to be the aggressor
So we can both be sure, no lesser.
So we can stick out
Our tongues, laugh
And maintain elegant friction.
I want to massage your body
Perfectly, head to toe, latent sin.
While holding your hand
With one condition:
Your consented bidding.
I want to slide into your beauty
Atop a blue pool table.
Place my hands on your hips.
Blue jeans and bare feet,
Dangling necklaces.
I want to be naked
In your presence
Within each other's premise.

VIRTUALITY

An open space.
Filled with lingering
Thoughts writ large
By zeros and ones.
Holograms, wholly engorged
Connected by electric pulse.
You're plugged in, tuned out,
At the mercy of an ungodly
Lover. Your ultimate weakness.
She, or he, at thy command.
Virtual happiness in vastness
Tenders uncertain ramifications
Beneath an everyday sky.
Find a lover in the cracks
Of reality, physical acts.
Then turn the power out.

I CAN'T TAKE IT

I can't take it.
I want to undress.
To bathe in your essence.
To howl into the night.
To pump in unison.
You drive me into a frenzy,
Touching, your precision.
And implore me to bare all:
The secrets and sins.
The passions and pleasures,
The blood uplifting.
We inhabit our skin.
We moan as one,
Building a crescendo.
Until the night seizes us.
Until we rage underwater.
Until we can't take it.
And the floodgates burst.
I can't take it.
We must twirl again.

ART MUSEUM AT THE EDGE OF THE UNIVERSE

Here we are.
Beyond space and time.
In our own Blue Zone.
Spectators smile and grin.
We paint and emit transmissions
So ecstatic, dogmatic signals
Singing past Sirius.
Brushstrokes and pressed breasts.
You and I.
Naked in life upon known shores.
We achieve within the frame,
Intending to be watched,
As we make love in a
Glass enclosure.
The inspiration, the creator's dream.
I'll pose for you anytime
At the art museum
At the edge of the universe.
Stroke your brush again,
We see everywhere.
Portals to a splendid union.
No delusion: We never end.

ENDLESS CREATION

The sun. The seed.
Stars, sperm and eggs
In the ether of creation.
On a sphere of love,
Trying to overcome,
Gases coalesce.
Before we reminisce
Imagine time's ages
Already past,
Already the future.
Worlds beget worlds.
Let's curate eternity,
Bathe in our own magma.

RELATIVITY

A hot stove or a pretty girl.
The latter makes time levitate,
Matter whisk away in a flash.
Destined for an infinite moon.
Einstein and apples.
Our gravity is binary.
A growing star when
Viewed from afar.
Beacon kisses.
Relativity is our design.

DRUNK IN PARIS

In the basement at 3 a.m.
La maison des étudiantes.
214 Boulevard Raspail.
Blond hair and black boots.
I don't even ask.
You've appeared.
Words escape use.
Pleasantries exchanged
In a common body language.
Will we remember?
Will I catch my flight?
You fall asleep naked on the
Red satin bed.
I spill your Bordeaux wine and
The story loops from the
Beginning, straight to no end.
Absinthe, a friend of mine,
But no female companion.
I have better things to attend.
Oubliez, oubliez...
Our clothes, needless.
The night isn't dead.

FANTASY GIRL

Oils, open mouths and ecstasy.
Worldly fuel or bodily splendor.
Love: the final solution.
Dine with me tonight.
Let me whisper in your ear.
Tell you sweet somethings.
Observe. A fly on our wall.
Smiles, longing glances
And unfilled glasses.
The piano calls.
Your voice, soprano,
Fills an empty room
With life
With desire.
With high-cheek-boned fire.
We sigh, dream and kiss.
Birthday suits, secrets,
Beaches and airplanes.
A whirlpool of sensual air.

DEATH BY SEX

Friends, lovers, confidantes.
We are a machine.
Constantly oiled.
Pistons and levers.
Pulleys and straps.
Blue perpetual motion
Connected to the sky
Of our carnal imagination.
Listen and learn.
To yearn, to give in.
Devastation in our wake.
For our sake, we partake.
And wonder why it took so long.

SOUTH OF FRANCE, NORTH OF HEAVEN

You stand still as time moves.
Your black bikini a paean
To something new.
The Republic of Beauty.
Dark hair and eyes. Lithe.
I want to undress my eyes
With you. Blinding the sun.
Room 1026 is only
Fifty yards away.
Across the road,
In another dimension.
A pedestal borne of
An eclectic heaven.
We're there before
We know it.
Grasping at clothes
Grasping for love.
One kiss and…

SAKURA

Snow in April,
Not a cold blast
But the wind-filled
Blossoms as we
Fall into each other.
Your lips pressed
Against mine beneath
A tree. Of life. Of love.
Besotted breath
Boldly dreaming.
Like floating petals
We try to make it last.

PAST LIFE

Meet me at the signpost.
Stark, in the after Eden,
There's no need for clothes.
There's no place for shame.
We are all one here.
Unbridled, loving freely.
However we like.
If you're still in the past life,
Project, heed the amorous urge.
Past life, nothing's guaranteed.
Waiting for release, imprison us.
Fear not, the door will open.

THE BOOK OF X

I cut myself on the pages of your book.
My deviant thoughts roused.
Your passion engorged.
Your papyrus, a call to action:
Our constitution.
I stand before you at will.
Pleasuring on command.
The deed is done, but we
Don't close the tome.
Clothes flung far and free.
Reading, rushing, rapture.
We fill new pages and new books.
We remain a companion piece.
A work of non-fiction.
Full of volume.
Opened to the same upturned
Corner over and over.
The world without end.
Author unknown.
Author's muse reborn.

LOGOMACHY

Escape. The argument flees
Out the open door.
A whistling sentience
Bound for oblivion.
Let the crevasse pass.
Engage in peculiar weather,
The storm generated in love.
The tenderness created by
The touch of a finger.
A genuine smile replacing all.
The things we don't say
Can do no harm.
Repay and make love.
Reclaim the naked spark
With savoring intent.
Linger longer. Hands intertwined.
If you want me here,
The words must never return.

BEAUTIFUL/TERRIBLE

It starts with the body.
Wells up from the tide.
The skeletons sting
Like needles in the ongoing
War of conquest.
Enemies have no chance.
Lovers even less.
Men, women, tears.
Skin lathered,
Foam, lotion and dandelion
The image burns, as your
Delights render terrible pain,
An unquenchable urge
Solved and salved by beauty,
The dichotomy, the insanity.
There is no cure.

ZERO FUCKS

The power rises.
At first, a strange daze.
Then clarity.
A realization.
Metastasized.
The less you care,
The more you dare.
The more insidious courage
Leads you to lustful love
And zero fucks.

POPSICLE

I'm melting.
Thinking of you
Dripping on
Somebody else.
I'll put on my three-piece
Blue suit and maybe
Somebody else
Will notice me,
Undress me
With their eyes.
A radiant shade
Of Green
Leaving a stain
On my breast.
While the juice
Withers in the sun.

QUESTIONS WITHOUT ANSWERS

Will you be mad if I ask
to make love to you?
Will you believe me when
I tell you you're beautiful?
Will you mind if I think about you
When I'm penetrating someone else?
Do you hold your head up
and rise to meet the sky?
If I hold your hand, will you let me?
And place my fingers
Where you want them to be?
Where does your heart reside?
Is it tucked away like one
Of our fleeting glances?
Will you let me pleasure you?
Do you enjoy staring at your
Body in the mirror?
Or do you prefer a warm fireplace
With an eager lover?
How long has it been?
Where are you now?
Will you think less of me

If I tell you my secrets?
Do silhouettes of our time together exist?
Will you wear those black jeans for me?
If we meet in a hotel room
What will happen?
Will you still be there in the morning?
What are we afraid of?

FREEDOM GODDESS

Stand and possess your power,
Feet wide apart beneath the trees
Amongst the other lovers,
Amongst the welcoming sky.
Amongst all the beautiful colors.

You are the paragon of pleasure.
There is no pain. Not yet.
That comes later when
You drive the next man (*or woman*) mad.
Nobody will see.

Walk the path others fear
Showered by luscious green leaves
And never judged.
Here's to the day you share
Your freedom with me.

THE DREAM II

This turbulent man needs dreams
To survive the long dark night,
The fleeting sleep on a spinning world
Filled with infinite delights, or one,
Depending on his inclination.
Heartache has a woman's name.
His reverie always begins on her lips while
Quivered tongues mask his true
Countenance in the shadows.
Contortions of mind and body
We fit together like missing pieces
Of a puzzle waiting to fall apart again.
Her muscles, beautiful chords.
Her brown eyes pull my body inward.
Toward her bosom, an exquisite haven.
When she touches me, I smile.
Knowing full well she will disappear
Before the sun releases us all.
Despite these facts,
The dream I cling to never ends.

BLACK HAIR, WHITE LACE

A picture, a place.
Visions worth a 1,000 nights.
Objects and abstractions.
Cream and divine light.
A halo of lust
Dusted by grace:
Your attraction.
Faultless thighs aligned,
Curved to engender delectation.
Fluid thoughts,
Embattled doubts.
Across an infinite field,
Your face in the doorway.
Black hair, white lace.

GIVE HER WHAT SHE WANTS

Stand at attention.
Bring your "A" self.
Replete with imagination,
And a plan.
Migrate toward the
Center of forever.
Ring in the New Year.
Chin up, blinds down.
Legs splayed.
Minds pierced.
True hearts
Will not be returned.
Give her what she wants.

THE TRUTH

Pain or pleasure.
Truth, lies,
Indifference.
Castigated
A final time.
Nothing matters.
Everything swirls.
I spy a tear
And reject it.
My mouth opens,
But no words escape.
You're already a whisper.
The wind's my enemy
Because of hallowed fact.
The truth is...I love you.

THE WORST KEPT SECRET
IN THE WORLD

We are all alone.
Alone among the stars.
Alone in the thick of night.
Silent reveries beg us,
Their shagging breaths
Titillate us, heaving bosoms,
Buttocks and the rest.
Fling the ether away,
Consume the combustible
Stasis of our joint combination.
The future is long past.
We are alone together,
Alone in our minds.
Alone in the pool hall of life.
Words, tokens, amulets.
Dangle from your neck.
Cleavage hewn from
Marbled excellence.
Rings ring true.
While sly smiles reveal
My wanting eye.
For clarity's sake:

My appetite for you is
The worst kept secret
In the world.

MAY I...

May I take you...
To the movies. To the beach.
To karaoke, your voice divine.
To dinner, unrelenting.
May I think nasty pleasantries?
Fast forward, hit pause, rewind.
May I kiss you beyond passion?
May I take off your clothes
As you take off mine?
May I forget our lives for
One, or infinite nights?
Touch, feel, marinate.
May I grow in your hands?
May I go down for as long
As you're willing? 24/7.
Taken, swept aside.
May I admire your beauty
In the last row?
Settled into a hard seat,
Listening to perfect pitch.
May I take you dancing?
Alluring fumes wafting.
Cheekbones and smiles,
May I take you?

A PIECE OF BROOKLYN

I met you on a dewy morning in the park.
Your sinews tied to mine in time.
The leaves golden, all out of line.
We were fleeting from the start,
A fantasy lived and maintained
For three short weeks.
Spirals of kisses preceded
The inevitable unreturned calls.
I'll remember you well,
The fall shadow that yields to the sun.
A piece of Brooklyn lodged
In my mind's sky.

RIGHT NOW YOU ARE PERFECT

Right now you are perfect.
We've made love
Countless times in theory.
Each time better than
The last but not the next.
We dream without argument
Before hatred and apathy seize
The reins. We reign in ecstasy.
Your body is perfect.
Your mind is perfect.
Your legs fill me with desire.
I place my hand on
The small of your back,
The nape of your neck.
Our breaths in rhythm.
I make all the right moves.
I am perfect.
You are perfect.
The signs are beautiful.
There is no fear.
A smile everlasting.
We joke, we sing, we hum.

I conjure every position.
We can lie naked in
Each other's arms
Without penetration
And be more intimate
Than if we insert our
Digits and keyholes
Everywhere in every city.
On each other
In synchronicity.
Massage our souls
For hours on end.
Wallow in our imperfection.
No fatigue, only elation.
We can release what we feel
Without recourse.
Without destruction.
Without end.
Love is the only repercussion.
In our imagination:
Right now we are perfect.

1,001 NIGHTS

Kill me with your stories.
Kill me with your dreams.
We'll lie together until dawn
And create our own steam.

Kill me with your body.
Kill me with your light.
We'll become one beast
And enjoy mortal sight.

Kill me with your kisses.
Kill me with your love.
We'll fly to nouveau heights
And frolic amongst doves.

Kill me with your eyes.
Kill me with your skin.
We'll embrace nude
And become sexual jinn.

Kill me with your desire.
Kill me with your might.
We'll continue this journey
And pierce flesh 1,001 nights.

EPILOGUE:
THERE IS ONLY ONE THING

There is only one thing.
There is only one answer.
There is only one smile.
There is only one heart.
There is only one cure.
There is only one mind.
There is only one peace.
There is only one love.
There is only one you.

ACKNOWLEDGMENTS

First and foremost, thank you to my family, which supersedes all the problems in the world. Thank you to anyone who has ever written, read or listened to a poem, and to those of you who are thinking about it. I believe the definition of poetry is subjective. It can be a single word, or a 50,000 line epic tale of free verse, or a painting, a glance, a film, a photograph, a sculpture, an amazing design, a play, a lover, a glass of milk or the glint in your children's eyes. Poetry is life and vice versa. I hope you enjoy this latest collection. These acknowledgments are a form of poetry in and of themselves. And please forgive me if I accidentally leave anyone (you) out. It wasn't intentional.

Thank you to Mom and Dad, who took home "the most beautiful baby at the baby store" (according to Mom). I am forever your son and forever grateful. To my wife, thank you for everything, especially for being a great mom. To our beautiful daughters, Kokomi and Momoka: thank you for the amount of love, laughter and joy you bring into our lives on a daily basis. Words don't even describe how blessed I am to have you and your mother in my life. Family is the most important thing. Also to everyone who has helped us take care of them, and continues to help, along the way (The Okitsu Family, Seevon Chau, Seema Sadanandan); to my brothers Brian and Chris, and their families, thank you for your love and support. To my late grandparents, Dr. and Mrs. Raymond J. Pitts, who taught me to work hard and Dream Big. Thank you to the Bias, Pitts and Smith Families. To family in Japan and Thailand, thank you for welcoming me with open arms. To my New York City and worldwide friends (in no particular order), thank you for your immeasurable help over the years and for inspiring me: Hiromi Saeki, Chilembwe Mason, Jim Chan, Robson Garcia (and family in Brazil), Chi Mac, Faisal Azam, Erica Velis, Jennymar, John Plenge, Paul Gutierrez, Kyle Errison, Karen Lee, Mike Heck, Armen Keteyian, Lars Anderson, Leslie Bornstein, Renate Jensen, Paul Tam, Naomi Castillo (congrats on the little one), Shui Chen, Lisa Darling, Joanne, Motoko, Joe Toris and everyone at MoMa; Ancel Bowlin, Scott Hevesy, Jaramay Aref, Gene Menez, Tracy Mothershed, Elizabeth Newman, Farrell Evans, Cory Calhoun, Karen Strauss, Karen Meneghin, Cynthia Cortes; the cast and crew of *Noctambulous* and all of my independent films; Everyone at *Sports Illustrated* (cktk only everyone), especially Gabe Miller, who still listens to my ideas—baked, half-baked and unbaked, as well as Richard Demak, Larry Mondi and librarians, Joy Birdsong, Natasha Simon and Susan Szeliga. The SI library on the 18th floor of the Time & Life Building is no more, but the memories exist eternally. Dimitry Léger, thank you for your friendship, suggestions, and paving the way with *God Loves Haiti*; Brian Jaramillo, who gave me my first journalism job at the *Arizona Daily Wildcat*; Everyone at the Minskoff and Brooks Atkinson Theaters; my friends and former colleagues at *The Dallas Morning News*; Alexei

Barrionuevo; Mrs. Pell, wherever you are, thank you for typing the stunted beginnings of my (still unpublished) first novel attempt, The Sword & Shield of Coromir, a blatant J.R.R. Tolkien ripoff; to my Cannes crew, Anne Vallersnes (and Nicolas and the girls), Sonja Kiefer, Bettina Meetz, João Serejo; to past loves and lovers; to the Disneyland crew, Kevin Gidden, Claudia Ancalmo and numerous others; my foster/godmother Jackie Bergman (now Gardner); Alan Tafoya; thank you to Marina and Jason Anderson of Polgarus Studio for formatting *Immaculate Dust*; Everyone at St. Matthias church in Whittier, California, The Cervantes Family, Sigur Family and Everyone on Light Street; Willie Joe Philbin and The Philbin Family, my friends, fraternity brothers and football teammates at the University of Arizona, my professors (especially Gary Garrison and Richard Wesley) and classmates at NYU. Thank you, the reader. And to all writers and fellow dreamers, keep writing and keep dreaming. Everyone has helped me on my journey as a writer, artist and human being. Thank you.

Sincerely,
Kelvin C. Bias, New York City, January 2019

OTHER WORK BY KELVIN C. BIAS

MILKMAN (Novel)

What happens when everyman Calder Boyd starts to lactate? The Manhattanite becomes a media cause célèbre nicknamed the Milkman and old and new problems spill forth. The son of a former NBA star and a Norwegian artist, Calder copes with his strained marriage, losing his copywriting job at a boutique ad agency, a male-empowerment espousing mailman and a porn-star performance artist who wants to exploit him. He also deals with his late father's legacy and his wife's past indiscretion — all while breastfeeding their newborn daughter. Calder eventually becomes a pawn in the battle between a feminist organization and a militant men's society as he tries to become a better husband and man. The Fourth Estate, sex, art, love, memory, marriage and family converge during the snowiest winter on record in this commentary on contemporary American fatherhood.

WHISPERS OF A DYING SUN (Poetry)

These poems represent the vestiges of man from the perspective of a distant future. Akin to radio signals, the remnants of humanity streak toward a black hole where art, politics, love, technology, philosophy, science and the yearning for eternity accrete. Prophetic, stoic, polyphasic, the words disassemble and recombine on the other side in search of a new sun. I hope these poems find a closer home in your personal universe, heard but you're unsure of their origin, like whispers.

SEXOPOLIS: POEMS ON LOVE AND SEX

Love is a liberation, an act, a rebellion, a restriction, a communion. This poetry collection covers the universal topics of love and sex. From erotic to platonic and from marital to familial, love comes in many forms. We don't always get it, but we all crave it.

ABOUT THE AUTHOR

Kelvin C. Bias is a journalist, novelist, poet, filmmaker and raconteur. However, his most important moniker is father. He lives in Brooklyn with his wife and daughters.

Immaculate Dust: Love Poems is his third poetry collection. Connect with Kelvin on Instagram & Twitter: @archivezero

www.ingramcontent.com/pod-product-compliance
Lightning Source LLC
LaVergne TN
LVHW021353080426
835508LV00020B/2254